The
SHADOW
of My
YOUTH
FOLLOWS ME

Poetry of an Adult Child of an Alcoholic
"A message of faith & forgiveness"

by

DEBORAH MCFARLIN HOBBS

Illustrations by Molly Hodgkiss

AuthorHouse™
1663 Liberty Drive
Bloomington, IN 47403
www.authorhouse.com
Phone: 833-262-8899

Because of the dynamic nature of the Internet, any web addresses or links contained in this book may have changed
since publication and may no longer be valid. The views expressed in this work are solely those of the author and do
not necessarily reflect the views of the publisher, and the publisher hereby disclaims any responsibility for them.

Any people depicted in stock imagery provided by Getty Images are models,
and such images are being used for illustrative purposes only.
Certain stock imagery © Getty Images.

Unless otherwise noted, Scripture quotations are taken from the Holy Bible, "New International Version", "NIV" Copyright ©
1973, 1978, 1984, 2011 by Biblica, Inc. Used by permission of Zondervan. All rights reserved worldwide. www.zondervan.com. The
"NIV" and "New International Version" are trademarks registered in the United States Patent and Trademark Office by Biblica, Inc.

Scripture quotations marked KJV are taken from the King James Version. Public domain.

This book is printed on acid-free paper.

ISBN: 979-8-8230-2313-9 (sc)
ISBN: 979-8-8230-2314-6 (e)

Library of Congress Control Number: 2024904386

Print information available on the last page.

Published by AuthorHouse 05/23/2024

authorHOUSE®

CONTENTS

DEDICATED TO

My Beloved Siblings:
Donna
Alfreda
Ray

and to all Adult Children of Alcoholics

ACKNOWLEDGEMENT

To the one who inspired me to write this book,
and supported me with the endeavor.
I am forever grateful to the love of my life, my husband,
Nelson

"God loves us too well, than for us to dwell,
in a self-made hell.
He'll see us through the storms of life,
and there are no storms in paradise".
-Deborah M Hobbs

INTRODUCTION

My name is Debbie, and I am an Adult Child of an Alcoholic. For most of my life, I have struggled with the feeling that my inner child follows me day after day, like a tormenting shadow, reminding me of my past traumatic upbringing.

While I was in counseling, I began writing poems as a form of therapy. I needed to confront the issues that plagued me, due to my father's alcoholism, and the negative impact it had on my life.

Alcoholism not only effects the one who abuses it, but it also effects the people who live with an abusive alcoholic, especially if the alcoholic is abusive to the people that they love. The scars left behind on children last well into adulthood. Post-Traumatic Stress Disorder, nightmares, flashbacks, anxiety, panic attacks, chronic depression, anger issues, fear, inability to trust and unforgiveness are common problems that Adult Children of Alcoholics may face.

There were many times when my family and I did not feel safe in our own home. We dreaded nights and weekends. We didn't know from one day to the next what to expect. Would he come home as Dr. Jekyll or Mr. Hyde? This generated a lot of confusion for a child. We all loved my father, but when he got intoxicated, he was like an entirely different person. He was an evil, angry, violent, and controlling man. The result was psychological and physical abuse, directed toward his family, primarily toward my mother. My siblings and I witnessed things during our childhood that no child should ever have to witness.

Sadly, this dysfunctional lifestyle was the norm for my mother because her father was an abusive alcoholic as well. Some of the things he did were inhumane, such as pulling planks on their porch and nailing children under them for hours, when they misbehaved, or putting a child's hands on a hot wooden stove for punishment.

Domestic violence was essentially ignored in the legal and medical fields until recent times. Societies response to an alcoholic battering his wife or abusing his children was perceived as a family problem and a private matter that needed to be worked out by the parties involved. It was not considered to be a criminal matter.

During that time, my mother could not get the help she needed to leave an abusive relationship. There were no shelters. She had four young children, no job, no money, and no place to go. She did not believe in divorce and wanted to keep her family together. My Dad also told her that he would kill her if she ever left. She was imprisoned by a life full of trauma, drama, sadness, and fear.

Today, there are more resources available to people in these situations; however, domestic violence, involving alcohol, remains a serious and tragic problem, sometimes resulting in great bodily injury or death.

Some statistics estimate that roughly 55% of domestic abuse perpetrators were drinking alcohol prior to an assault.

If you are living with a violent alcoholic, please get help! If you are in a dangerous situation, get out if you can! Tell someone. Get the support that you need and deserve.

With God's help, the writing of this book has enabled me to turn pain into purpose and to vaporize the shadow of my youth. It has freed me to forgive my father after all these years. For other Adult Children of Alcoholics, I pray that with God's help, you too will be able to forgive your parent, or the one who hurt you, and that the tormenting shadow of your past will forever flee.

A CHILD'S SHADOW

When I wake up, what do I see?
a child's shadow that follows me.
A sad little girl in her own little world
trying to make sense of it all

She doesn't understand.
She can't comprehend.
Her uncertainty bothers me,
this child that follows me.

She's been there all my life.
I feel her pain and strife.
She's such a troubled girl,
so lonely in her world.

I cannot run from her.
She appears out of nowhere.
I wish she'd go away,
and not follow me every day.

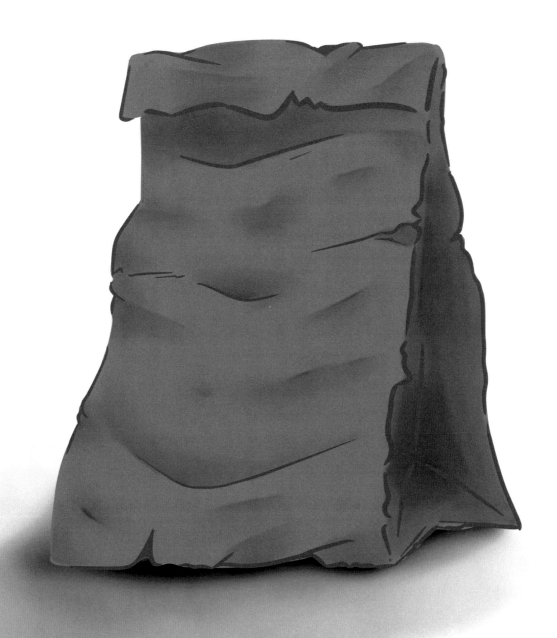

BROWN PAPER BAG

I remember –
We all had to keep
a change of clothes
in a brown paper bag,
hidden in the closet.
We had to be ready
to grab it
when we had to run
from Daddy.

CRAVING

There was a baby girl, born into this world,
not knowing how her life would be.
She was born with complications,
Her parents were by her side,
praying for God to keep her alive.
Her father made a promise to God;
If she lived, he would stop drinking.
What on earth was he thinking?
That very night, he hid a bottle under her bed.
His craving for alcohol had to be fed.
So hard to understand,
the cravings of this man.

DEMONS

The demons of my past reside
within the corners of my mind.
They think my mind is a playground
for evilness, sight, and sound.

They were born of a curse.
They torture my mind and worse;
they damage my health,
and lower my esteem of self.

The gut-wrenching pain of my past
and flashbacks coming so fast
from the days gone by,
when my father was high.

FAITH

She never lost hope when it was all uphill.
She kept the faith and her strong will.
Though living with him was hard to do;
her faith in God was always true.

Mom prayed for Dad for many years.
At the altar she shed so many tears.
Some say she was a "tough old bird."
Day and night, she read God's word.

Her prayers were many, throughout her life.
She lived a sad life, as his wife.
But her life taught us about faith in God,
and to never lose hope when times are hard.

She stuck to the fight when she was hardest hit.
Throughout her sad life, she never quit.
She had a forgiving heart, we always knew.
Faith was the reason she made it through.

FAMILY

What's a family supposed to be like?
Are they happy or do they argue and fight?
When the dad comes home from work,
does he stagger in the door,
and throw a knife in the wall or floor?
Do the children run and play,
or from their Dad run away?
Do they feel safe at home,
or do they feel they don't belong?

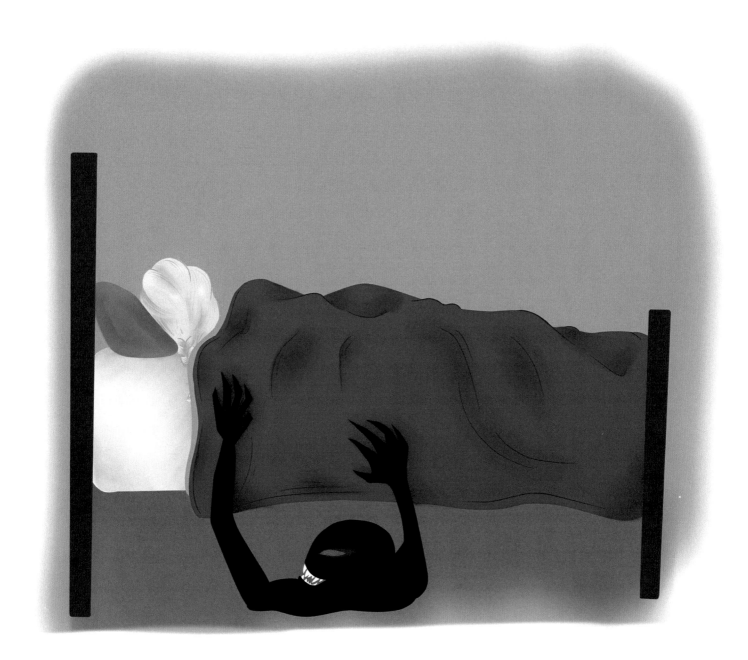

FEAR

Ever present fear,
why do you come near?
I once ran from you.
I know what I must do.
I first met you in my youth.
So hard it is to face the truth.
You came to me in a dream one night,
and awakened me with a scream of fright.
Sometimes you're in disguise,
but you always bring lies.
Ever present fear,
you're not welcome here.
Be gone to you, I shout!
In Jesus' name, get out!

FIRE

Don't be led astray
by choices you make each day.
There's a lot at stake
from the choices you make.
Be wise and open your eyes.
Don't abuse drugs or drink;
it's a terrible mistake.
Of all the things I've learned,
touch fire, and you'll get burned!

FORGIVE

Daddy, I want to forgive you
for the things that you did,
for the times that you hurt me,
for the things that you said.

I don't know if you remembered,
but you called me bad names.
I was only eight years old,
and it caused me such shame.

You hurt my self-confidence.
You lowered my self-esteem.
You said I'd never amount to anything
and caused me to falsely believe.

All of the things you did or said,
I know it wasn't really you.
It was the alcohol you drank Dad.
I can't forget, but I forgive you.

GETTING LATE

It's dark outside.
We've all gone to bed.
It's summertime,
but quilts cover our head.

He's still not home.
It's getting late.
We should all be asleep,
but we lay wide awake.

We lay there waiting,
We pretend we're asleep.
When he comes home,
we can't even speak.

It's going to be
one of those nights,
cursing and screaming,
fussing and fights.

This place we call home,
It gets scary here –
where evil lurks,
Satan's drinking a beer.

The screams get louder.
The children start to cry.
We don't understand,
but we can't ask why.

It's getting all quiet now.
Morning has broken.
At the breakfast table,
no words are spoken.

We get ready for school,
A new day begins,
but come nighttime,
We will do it again.

HOW COULD HE HAVE KNOWN?

How could he have known what he'd put us through?
Why did he do it to his loved ones, if he only knew?
How could he have known that he would turn out to be
this man who was feared by his own family?
How could he have known the price we'd have to pay,
for the memories that would haunt us each and every day?
How could he have known that he could have killed our mother?
Not only her, but me, my sisters, and my brother
How could he have known that we would often run and hide?
He may come home as Dr. Jekyll; but we prayed, not Mr. Hyde.
How could he have known when he drank his liquor or beer,
that it would cause all of our hearts to fear?
This Mr. Hyde, with the devil inside, knew just what he would do;
but, then I paused, and realized Doctor Jekyll lived in him too.
The answer is in the question; I guess he never knew.

HURT

Sometimes the very ones you love the best,
hurt you the most.
They love you too,
but they can do more damage hurting you
than anyone else in this world can ever do.

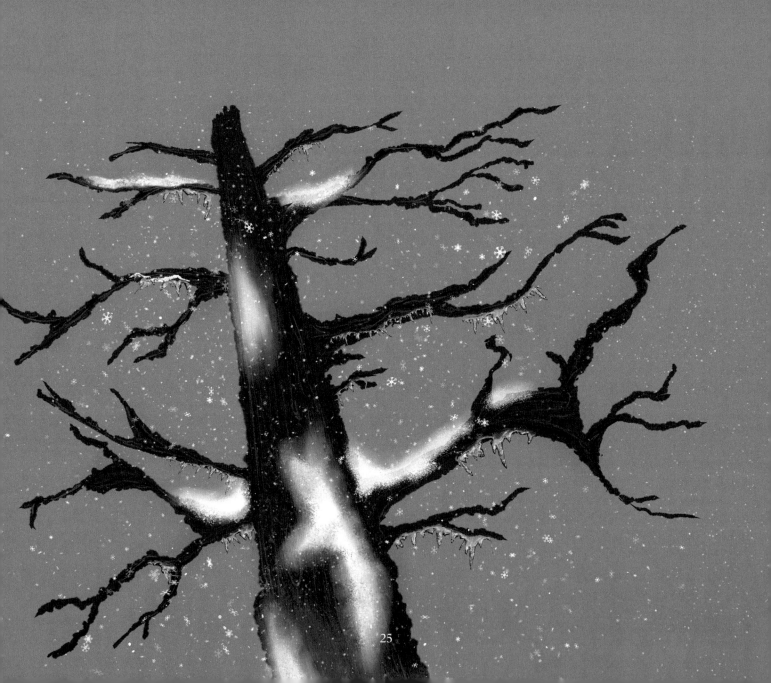

25

I CANNOT FEEL

Sounds of silence scream my name.
The hurt is real, but I feel no pain.
I am alone in a crowd.
The quiet voice is so loud.

I sleep while I'm standing and run while I sit.
A punch in my face feels like a kiss.
I cannot feel what is real.
My childhood you did steal.

The grass is blue, and the sky is green.
Your love for me cannot be seen.
The frost on the trees doesn't melt.
Your hugs cannot be felt.

I WANTED

I wanted to have friends over.
I wanted to have some fun.
I wanted to run in clover,
and play out in the sun.

I wanted to laugh, not cry.
I wanted to have a sleep over.
I wanted him to live, not die.
I wanted my Dad to be sober.

I wanted to be a little girl,
not a child in a grownup world.
But now he's gone,
and this child is grown.

I WISH

By: Donna M Whitfield

Daddy, I wish your childhood was better.
I wish mine was too.
I wish you didn't have bad memories.
I wish I didn't too.
I wish Mama didn't have to live in such turmoil in the past.
I wish I didn't too.
I am thankful for the good times my mom has had in the past few years.
She still misses you.
I do too.
I wish you had known my children.
You would have loved them.
I hope you have found peace Daddy.
I love you.

LETTER TO DAD

I know your life was filled with pain.
We all know you weren't too blame.
You struggled with your addiction.
It was a disease that caused your affliction.

I'm sorry that you carried this burden Dad.
It hurt you so much and it makes me sad
for what you went through in your life.
You had so many hard times, sickness, and strife.

But now you're no longer suffering.
You're in Heaven where angels sing, and Christ is King.
Dad, I can't wait to see you again. I'll hold your hand,
As we walk streets of gold in that far away land.

MOMMA'S TEARS

Why couldn't Momma cry?
She didn't even know why.
She had to be strong for so long.
I guess her tears just dried up.
She had cried long enough.
My precious Momma wanted to cry.
Daddy's drinking caused her such pain.
Tears should have poured like rain,
but not one drop fell from her eyes.
It had nothing to do with her pride.
It had all to do with her numbness inside.
She couldn't reveal what she couldn't feel.

MOTHER

For every prayer that she has said
Every tear that she has shed
For every dream that she has dreamed
For every light she has gleamed
For every moment we have shared
For every care that she has cared
For every game that she has played
Every time that she has stayed
For every song that she has sung
Every dinner bell she has rung
For every blessing she has given
Every lesson about living
For all the money that she's given me
Every mistake she has forgiven me
For every item she crocheted
Every bed of mine she made
For all the boo boos she made better
For every card and every letter
For all the wisdom she has taught me
Every item she has bought me
For all the times that she has rocked me

And should have but didn't sock me
For every kiss and every hug
For every blessing from above
For every meal that she has made
Every keepsake she has saved
For always showing me
What a strong woman can be
For every church service we attended
My hurts and broken heart she mended
For all she taught me about God
For every road that we have trod
For every place we went together
For every storm that we have weathered
For all the faith that she has had
For comforting me when I was sad
For being my best friend
Time and time again
For everything she's done for me
And for our family
The kind of mother I want to be

MY PIANO

Black and white keys on my piano,
played a song that Daddy knew.
I played it loud and clear,
as he sat there with his beer.

Playing a song on my piano,
that melody is a memory.
Playing it loud, playing it long,
that old familiar song.

I played upon my piano.
Please leave Momma alone!
I will play all night
to avoid a fight.

My heart and soul are in it.
Let me play, let me sing
the hymns from long ago,
songs that we both know.

Let me sing for you.
Let me play on my piano.
Please leave her alone!
Just listen to a song.

She had a moment of peace,
as Daddy and I sat at my piano.
I placed my fingers on the keys,
and he began to sing with me.

That old upright piano
almost had him in a trance.
Playing songs, and I knew
what the power of music could do.

NIGHT SKY

Oh, I remember the night sky,
when I'd look out my window and cry.
The tears that filled my eyes,
were no surprise.

When evening shadows fell,
and our home became a hell,
I'd see night sky and cry.
To God I would cry, …why?

I didn't understand
the meaning of God's plan.
I'd wish upon a star,
but the star was just too far.

Oh, I wanted to escape
the terror of our fate
to the starry, starry sky
where angels fly.
Night sky

NO FOOD

Momma is so worried. We have no food to eat.
When Daddy is drunk, he always wants meat.
We can't go to the store; the money is gone.
The pantry and frig are dry as a bone.

We ran next door and went inside.
The neighbors had gone out for a ride.
We went to the kitchen; what did we see?
We saw their pantry was full as could be.

They probably won't mind if we get a can or two;
pinto beans and potatoes will do.
Momma had some cornbread; she'd made a pone.
Daddy is in the driveway now, blowing the horn.

He gets out of the car, and he wants to know
what's for supper, as he staggers through the door.
The children had already set down to eat,
then he raises his voice cursing, where's the meat?

Momma said, we didn't have the money to buy
As a solitary tear fell from her eye.
He got so mad and cursed up a storm.
I hated the day that man was born.

In a fit of anger,
he picked up one end of the table,
then everything fell to the floor.
Food, tea, broken glass, and our meal was no more.

Then he grabbed her and pushed her down.
He was snarling with an evil frown.
His vulgar words of choice said clean up this mess
as her broken spirit was put to the test.

43

OK?

Momma, are you ok?
Did Daddy hurt you again?
I hate him for what he does.
The name calling, those bruises and blood
Why? Just because?
No! I know why.
It's only when he's high.
I wish he would stop drinking,
and all his cussing and hating.
Why can't he see that you're not ok?
Neither am I.

REALITY

Reality is a fantasy.
Vulgarity is a symphony.
Discipline is feared.
My eyes are full of tears.

Awakened in the dead of night,
Just to see my parents' fight.
He's to blame we live in shame.
Weekends are always the same.

Our neighbors know
because he puts on a show.
Abuse of liquor and beer
is the cause of our fear.
Living in an alcoholic home is not easy.

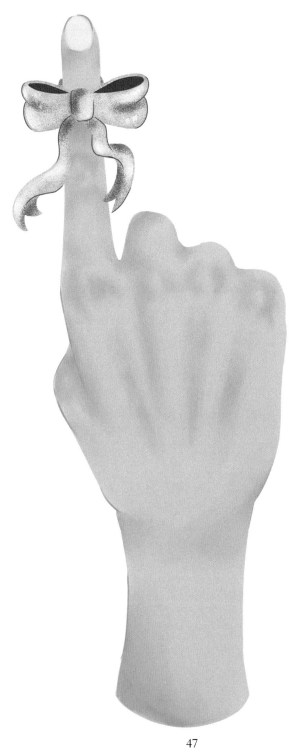

REMEMBERING

Remembering what I want to forget,
those dreaded nights and weekends,
of a childhood forever spent.
It was a common occurrence,
running and hiding from him.
Only a mother's reassurance,
could we make it through again.
Her faith and prayers got us through
those really bad days.
Now we give God the glory and praise!

SINS OF OUR FATHERS

I'm thinking of my Dad
and about the sins of his father.
Confront him? I didn't bother.
Why was Dad such a troubled man?
Did he know that God had a plan?
Why did he have to live that life?
He caused so much fear and strife.
It breaks my heart to know the pain
that he went through, and who's to blame?
I wish I'd had that talk with him
about his past and his father's sin.

SO VERY TALL

I watched her all my life.
She was so strong.
She didn't even cry.
I tried to understand why.
I watched as she was abused,
beaten, put down and used,
but her prayers got her through it all.
When she bowed on her knees,
she stood so very tall.

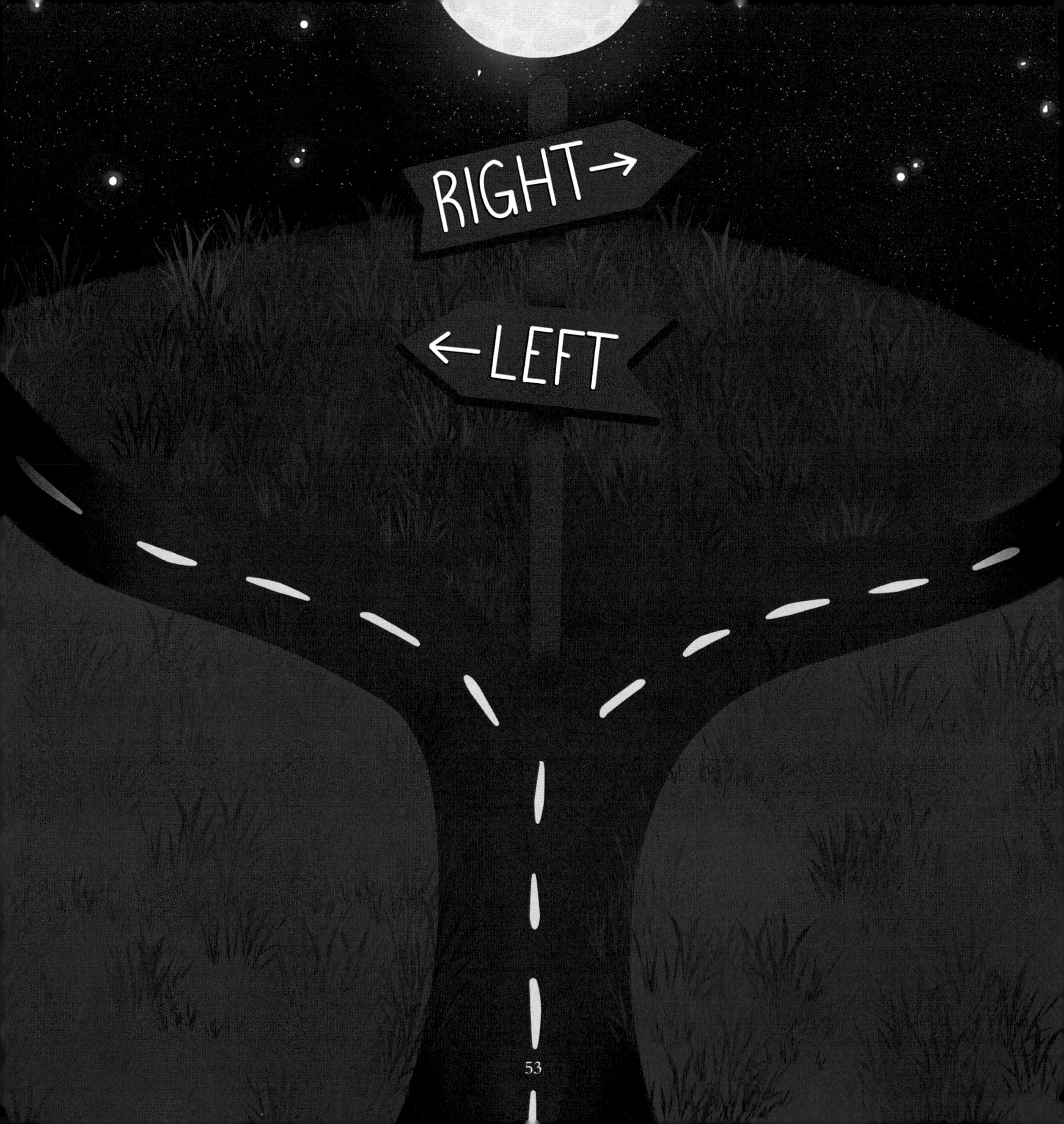
RIGHT→
←LEFT

SOMETIMES

The paths of my past were not all of my choosing.
I would have taken the other road if I could have,
but fate as it was, put me on that path.
I often wondered why God did allow it –
not only for me, but our whole family.
Sometimes I still break down and cry.

STORMS

Storms of life come and go.
Alcohol rains on my soul.
My father's addiction lives on,
long after he's dead and gone.
Some family members may feel defeated.
Generational curses are being repeated.
We don't always know why,
but on God, we must rely.
He'll see us through the storms of life.
and there are no storms in paradise.

TAKE A BOW

Nights of terror, fits of rage,
Who is this man upon the stage?
A demon lives inside our home.
A beer in hand, he starts to roam.
Throwing things in the night.
Children crying, filled with fright,
No way to leave, we can't escape.
Is it too late? He's planned our fate.
We run so hard to get away.
His foul mouth yells, you will stay.
It feels like a skit in a horror film.
I wonder if the devil is him.
I've seen him then; I see him now.
He takes off his mask and wipes his brow,
Then my father takes a bow.

THAT QUIET SOBER MAN

I wish I had really known him,
that quiet sober man inside.
I often wondered about him.
What did he have to hide?

We rode to work together,
only talked about the weather.
No substance to our words,
It was all on his terms.

That quiet sober man in our home,
sitting there so alone.
Trying to show us love,
but often fell short of.

THE CURSE OF MY FATHER

The curse of my father
tormented him throughout his life.
It affected his entire family,
especially my mom, his wife.

He drank away his paycheck,
but expected meat every meal.
My mother would scrimp and save
to provide a life that was real.

THE FLASHLIGHT

It's time to do my homework,
but he made us go to bed.
I have tests tomorrow,
and books I haven't read.

I said, I need to study Dad.
I've got so much to do,
but to him, it didn't matter
He did not have a clue.

I took my books and flashlight,
and covered up my head.
I tried my best to study,
as I laid there in my bed.

I found it hard to concentrate.
I tried to do my best.
He kept us up until very late.
I prayed to pass my test.

I didn't think I could do it.
I dreaded that next day,
but I managed to get through it,
and even made an 'A'.

THE OLD PIER

The old pier near my home on the lake
was my way of an escape.
I loved to swim and get a tan,
play 'king of the pier', with my siblings and friends.

It was so much fun,
just lying in the sun.
Songs of the seventies were on our radio.
Across the lake was a giant gazebo.

Big houses and trailers, fast cars, and old trucks
Some pinching pennies, some with a million bucks
The cove separated the rich from the poor,
but the lake let us be divided no more.

My Dad and I fished for brim.
It's where I learned to swim.
I loved that old pier; it's now washed away,
but deep in my heart, good memories will stay.

THE SHERIFF

She tolerated the intolerable, with no protection at all.
No laws against domestic violence, and no one to call,
No safe houses, no place to run to,
Not much that she could do.
We called the Sheriff, he said it's a family problem,
and he wasn't the one to solve them.

69

THEY SAY

They say time has a way of healing.
Well, if it's true, how long will I keep hurting?
How long will I feel this gnawing pain?
This pain that never goes away,
It's already been over sixty years.
Has that not been enough time to heal?
Enough time to stop the hurt that I carry
from these awful memories?
They say time has a way of healing.
What do they know?

TOO LATE

I can't go to sleep tonight.
Flashbacks in my head
Hiding under the cover
Thinking of things, you did

I wish I could have told you
before you left so soon,
the heartache that you caused
But there seemed no opportune.

In retrospect, I could of –
"could of", "would of", "should of",
but it's too late to do it now.
Even if it wasn't,
I wouldn't know how.

TROUBLE ME

Days gone by
but I still see
the things you did
to trouble me.

I replay things
night and day.
Please help me
Dear Lord, I pray.

I close my eyes
and when I sleep,
You haunt me.
My pain is deep,

so deep inside
I want to cry.
There's no escape,
except to die.

The sleepless hours
take a toll on me.
You'll never know;
You'll never see
the things you did
to trouble me.

WOUNDED CHILD

This wounded child I carry
within my heart and mind.
The burden is so heavy.
Some days, I can't stop crying.
She lives inside my body.
She's with me all the time.
Like a shadow that follows me,
This wounded child's still a part of me.

WRITTEN IN RED

I dipped my pen in black in just to say,
Dear Lord, help me with truth to convey
a message that human hearts comprehend.
then God allowed me to write with His pen.

Where do I start, dear Lord I pray?
Tell them that I am the Truth and the Way.
Sorrow will come, and in their life much fear,
with mine own Hand, I'll *erase* every tear.

You know what God wants you to do.
Accept His gift, Jesus died for you.
Don't wait too late, no decision made,
Because in time, this ink may fade.

I dipped my pen in God's ink just to say,
Dear Lord, help me *erase* mistakes I've made.
He said, precious child, repent, believe in me,
then He cast my sins into the forgotten sea.

With pen in hand, the ink began to flow,
and I thought of **His blood** shed for me long ago.
Sounds came to me like a great symphony.
Do you hear them too? It's our Savior's plea.

You know what God wants you to do.
Accept His gift, Jesus died for you.
Don't wait too late, no decision made,
With time, this ink may fade.

Then I saw Him pick up the Lamb's Book of Life
Took His pen dipped in **red**
and my name He did write.
My name He did write.

CONCLUSION

I struggled most of my life with unforgiveness toward my father because of his alcoholism and abusiveness to my mother and our family. For so many years, I was only hurting myself by not forgiving him. There is nothing good that can come from unforgiveness. I recognized that I could either be bitter or better from my past hurts. This didn't mean that I would forget what happened; that would be humanly impossible. It meant that I could **choose to forgive.**

So, what does it really mean to forgive someone? It simply means that we will accept what has happened and move on, with God's help. It is all about choices and turning things over to a loving God.

You may be suffering because you haven't come to a point to where you can forgive the one who has hurt you due to alcoholism or some other reason.

Make a choice to turn it over to God for help so that it will not continue to ruin your life and potentially the life of your offspring. He 'll take away the bitterness that is within, if you will just let Him.

We know that the Bible teaches us that we are to **forgive in order to be forgiven** and if we don't forgive then our Father who is in heaven won't forgive us.

[14] "For if you forgive other people when they sin against you, your heavenly Father will also forgive you. [15] But if you do not forgive others their sins, your Father will not forgive your sins." Matthew 6:14-15 (NIV)

Nothing that we have ever gone through in this life that seems unforgivable is worth dying without God's forgiveness.

My father died at 65 years of age in 1991 with cancer, due to asbestosis. He weighed 80 pounds and suffered greatly before he died. He was saved three months before he died. He asked God for forgiveness, and he asked our family to forgive him.

As he lay there dying and with our family beside him, we began to say his favorite Bible passage, the 23rd Psalm, "The Lord is my Shepherd". The last words he heard before he took his final breath was, "and I shall dwell in the house of the Lord forever".

Some people say that if a person knows they are going to die, they will easily accept Christ as their Lord and Savior and ask Him for forgiveness. This is not true.

In the Bible, we find that when Jesus was crucified, there were two thieves hanging on a cross beside Him. One thief would not accept Him even though he was dying. Then, the other thief asked Jesus to remember him.

43 Jesus answered him, "Truly I tell you, today you will be with me in paradise."
Luke 23:43 (NIV)

"If we confess our sins, he is faithful and just and will forgive us our sins and purify us from all unrighteousness." *I John 1:9 (NIV)*

In fact, God will remember our sins no more. Our sins will not have any bearing on our salvation. God will cast our sins into the sea of forgetfulness.

As long as we are alive, there is still time to ask God for forgiveness, but don't wait until it is too late! We do not know when we will breathe our last breath.

"For I will be merciful to their unrighteousness, and their sins and their iniquities will I remember no more." *Hebrews 8:12 (KJV)*

In the winter of my mother's life, she found peace and joy. She didn't harbor bitterness toward my father. She prayed for him her whole married life.

Had it not been for her relationship with God, I don't believe she would have survived all those years of abuse at the hands of my father. She was such an amazingly strong woman of unwavering faith. She lived to see her prayers answered when my father accepted Jesus Christ as his Savior and Lord. My precious mother lived to be 92 years young and went to heaven almost exactly 30 years to the day after my father died. After she passed away in 2021, we literally found thousands of prayers she had written. She journaled her prayers for over four decades. It was unbelievable! She was a true prayer warrior and left behind an amazing legacy.

My mother's life taught me the importance of prayer and the hope of heaven. ***Her life taught me to have faith in God.*** She taught her children and grandchildren to rely on God for everything and to never lose hope no matter what the circumstances are.

She once said, ***"I have searched my whole life for a perfect person and a perfect place. Jesus is that person and heaven is that place."***

My father's life taught me about God's forgiveness. What man cannot forgive, God can. The life that my father lived has made me realize that if God can forgive him for all the things that he did to my mother, my sisters, my brother, and me; I know without a doubt that God can forgive me for my sins. If you don't know Christ as your Savior and Lord, He can forgive you too, if you just ask Him. He wants us to repent of our sins and be free from our past.

"For all have sinned and come short of the glory of God." Romans 3:23 (KJV)

We need to find meaning in our suffering. If we don't understand it, then it really makes it hard to forgive. I believe that our family suffered due to a generational curse, also knows as a bloodline curse or ancestral sin. For many years, the curse of alcoholism has passed down through our family's bloodline from one generation to the next, due to rebellion or sin against God. This curse affected the trajectory of our lives. When there is a reoccurrence of sin in a family, such as alcoholism, it is because someone in the family tree, has allowed sin to take root in their life and never repented or turned away from that sin. When this occurs, evil spirits permeate our lives. Family members are subjected to that sin and the door is open for an evil spirit to come into another life. Ancestral curses can destroy an individual, a family or an entire generation and even many generations to follow.

What does the Bible say about generational curses? Generational curses are a result of sin whereby God punishes the children and their children for the sin of the parents.

[18] "The Lord is slow to anger, abounding in love and forgiving sin and rebellion. Yet he does not leave the guilty unpunished; he punishes the children for the sin of the parents to the third and fourth generation." Numbers 14:18 (NIV)

We see that generational curses are real, and they will continue to manifest themselves upon individuals and families unless the curse is broken by repenting of our sins in the name of Jesus Christ. Repenting is to turn away from sin and not repeat it again and again, while knowing that it is wrong.

When a parent has a sinful lifestyle, the children are more likely to practice the same sinful lifestyle. Implied in the warning of Exodus is the fact that the children will choose to repeat the sins of their fathers.

[5] "You shall not bow down to them or worship them; for I, the Lord your God, am a jealous God, punishing the children for the sin of the parents to the third and fourth generation of those who hate me, [6] but showing love to a thousand generations of those who love me and keep my commandments." Exodus 20:5-6 (NIV)

God wants us to live a joyful and obedient life. Satan wants just the opposite, he wants a generational curse to continue to bring hurt and pain in our life, the lives of our family and our future generations.

My life was filled with unforgiveness, yet it held within it, a lesson of *faith and forgiveness.* It held within it, the power of prayer to our loving Father God, who is faithful and just to forgive us, no matter what mistakes we make, or how badly we are hurt by others. God loves us that much.

Printed in the United States
by Baker & Taylor Publisher Services